Handmade
HOLIDAY CRAFTS

Handmade CHRISTMAS Crafts

By Ruth Owen

Gareth Stevens
PUBLISHING

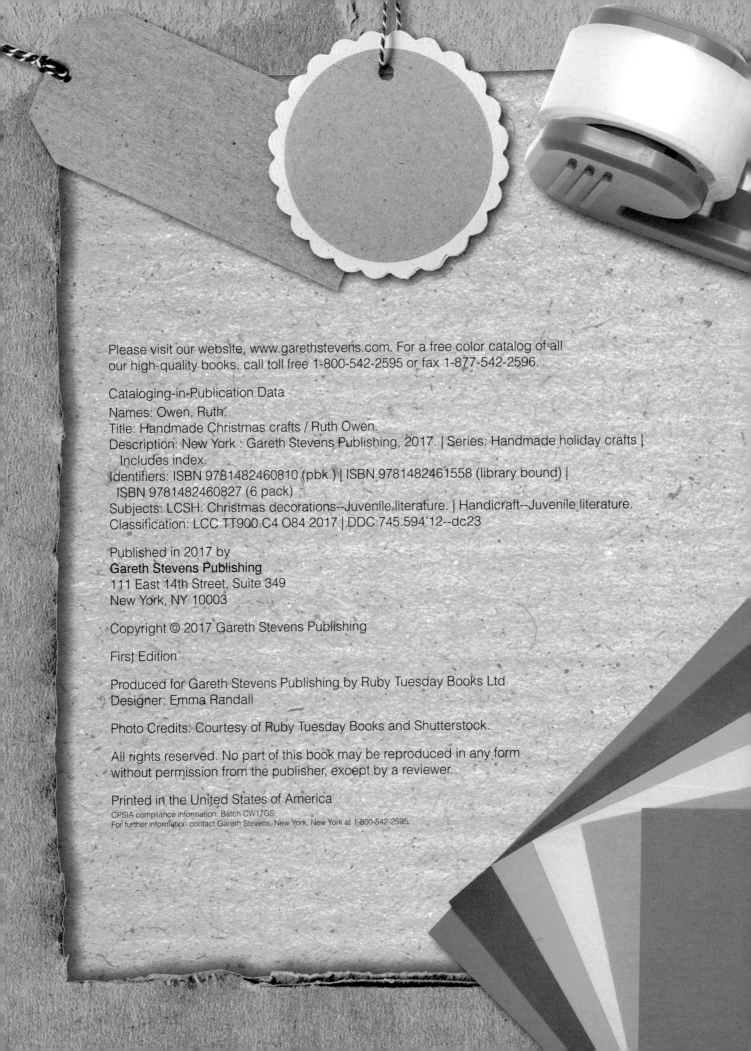

Please visit our website, www.garethstevens.com. For a free color catalog of all
our high-quality books, call toll free 1-800-542-2595 or fax 1-877-542-2596.

Cataloging-in-Publication Data

Names: Owen, Ruth.
Title: Handmade Christmas crafts / Ruth Owen.
Description: New York : Gareth Stevens Publishing, 2017. | Series: Handmade holiday crafts |
    Includes index.
Identifiers: ISBN 9781482460810 (pbk.) | ISBN 9781482461558 (library bound) |
    ISBN 9781482460827 (6 pack)
Subjects: LCSH: Christmas decorations--Juvenile literature. | Handicraft--Juvenile literature.
Classification: LCC TT900.C4 O84 2017 | DDC 745.594'12--dc23

Published in 2017 by
Gareth Stevens Publishing
111 East 14th Street, Suite 349
New York, NY 10003

First Edition

Produced for Gareth Stevens Publishing by Ruby Tuesday Books Ltd
Designer: Emma Randall

Photo Credits: Courtesy of Ruby Tuesday Books and Shutterstock.

Printed in the United States of America
CPSIA compliance information: Batch CW17GS:
For further information contact Gareth Stevens, New York, New York at 1-800-542-2595.

CONTENTS

A HAPPY HANDMADE HOLIDAY

When Christmas comes around, the stores are filled with beautiful, but sometimes expensive, decorations and holiday gifts.

This year, try the projects in this book and you'll soon be making your own holiday decorations and gifts using inexpensive crafting supplies and scraps of **recycled** materials from around your home.

All you need to do is follow the instructions, throw in a little of your own **creativity**, and you'll soon be having a very happy handmade holiday!

STAY SAFE

It's very important to have an adult around whenever you do any of the following tasks:

- Use scissors
- Use a glue gun
- Use an oven

4

YOU WILL NEED:

To make the projects in this book, you don't need any special equipment—just some basic crafting tools and supplies:

- Scissors
- Duct tape
- Glue gun
- White glue
- Paints and paintbrushes
- Sticky tape

RECYCLED CHRISTMAS DOOR WREATH

When Christmas comes around, it's **traditional** to welcome friends and family to your home with a colorful door wreath. Using leaves made from recycled plastic containers, you can create a funky, weatherproof, **environmentally friendly** holiday wreath for your door.

YOU WILL NEED:

- A large piece of cardboard slightly bigger than a dinner plate
- A dinner plate
- A saucer
- A pencil or a marker
- Scissors
- Duct tape
- A small piece of cardboard
- Colorful plastic containers such as yogurt and juice cartons, soda bottles, and foil containers
- A glue gun

1 To make a frame for the wreath, place a dinner plate upside down on the large piece of cardboard. Draw around the plate. .

2 Now place a saucer upside down in the circle you've just drawn. Draw around the saucer. You should now have a doughnut shape drawn on the cardboard.

3 Cut out the doughnut-shaped wreath frame. Wrap the frame in duct tape so that it is weatherproof.

4 To make the leaves for the wreath, begin by drawing a leaf template on a piece of cardboard. Cut out the template.

Template

5 Cut up your plastic or foil containers into flat pieces that are slightly bigger than the leaf template.

6 Place the leaf template onto a piece of carton and draw around it. Cut out the leaf.

7 Repeat step 6 until you have cut out about 120 leaves. This is the number you will need to cover a wreath frame that's the size of a dinner plate.

8 Using a hot glue gun, squeeze a small blob of glue onto the wreath frame. Then press the base of a leaf onto the glue. Be very careful not to touch the hot glue with your fingers.

9 Keep adding leaves to the frame. Slightly overlap the leaves to create a 3D effect. Angle the outer and inner leaves to create a traditional wreath shape.

10 When the frame is completely covered with leaves, it is ready to be hung on your door.

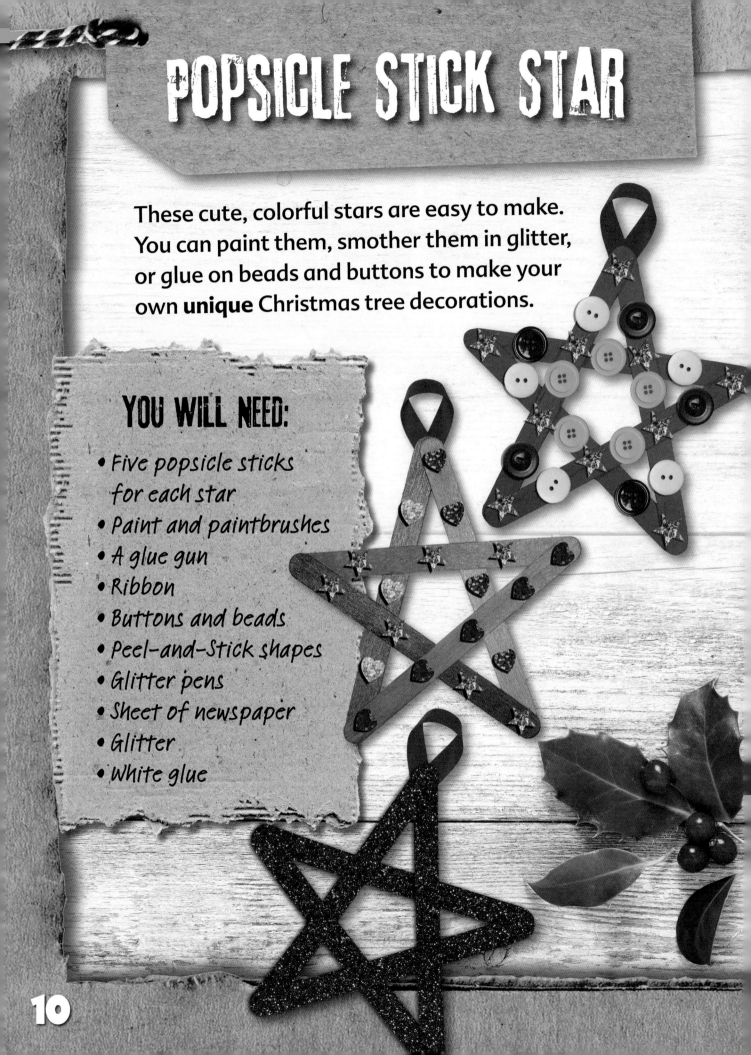

POPSICLE STICK STAR

These cute, colorful stars are easy to make. You can paint them, smother them in glitter, or glue on beads and buttons to make your own **unique** Christmas tree decorations.

YOU WILL NEED:

- Five popsicle sticks for each star
- Paint and paintbrushes
- A glue gun
- Ribbon
- Buttons and beads
- Peel-and-Stick shapes
- Glitter pens
- Sheet of newspaper
- Glitter
- White glue

1 Take five sticks and paint them your chosen base color.

You can buy popsicle sticks online or from craft supply stores. They are also known as craft sticks.

2 Use a glue gun to construct the star. Connect the sticks in the following order.

3 Next, glue a loop of ribbon to the top point of the star.

4 Now, get creative adding decorations to your star.

Peel-and-stick shapes

Glue on buttons

Add decorative squiggles
with glitter pens

5 You can also make a glitter star. Lay out
a sheet of newspaper. Cover one side of
your star with white glue.

6 Now sprinkle glitter over
the star. Allow the glue to
dry for about 30 minutes
and then shake off the
excess glitter.

YARN CHRISTMAS TREE

These cute yarn Christmas trees can be hung as decorations or used to decorate homemade Christmas cards. Just get winding to create your own unique woolen trees.

YOU WILL NEED:

- Cardboard
- Scissors
- Yarn in your choice of colors
- Tape
- Colorful beads

1 Cut a triangle shape from a piece of cardboard.

This project is a great way to recycle unwanted cardboard. For example, turn an old cereal box into Christmas trees.

2 Tape the end of some green yarn close to the base of the triangle.

3 Now, start wrapping green yarn tightly around the triangle to form the base layer of the yarn tree.

4 You can wrap the yarn in neat lines, or twist and turn the cardboard triangle to create a pattern or "messier" effect. When the tree is covered, tightly tuck the end of the yarn under the earlier layers at the back.

5 Now wind different-colored strands of yarn around the tree. Again, tuck all loose ends at the back under earlier layers.

6 To make mini tree decorations, thread some beads onto pieces of yarn and wind this yarn around the tree, too.

7 You can use your yarn trees to make handmade Christmas cards.

Merry Christmas

8 You can also make a decorative garland by attaching your trees to a length of string using wooden clothespins.

NO-SEW SOCK SNOWMAN

As long as you have a sock, some rice, and can tie knots, you can make this fantastic snowman decoration!

YOU WILL NEED:

To make one snowman
- A white sports sock
- Scissors
- White cotton string
- A roll of tape
- Dry, uncooked rice
- Fabric scrap to make a scarf
- Glue gun
- 3 buttons
- 3 pins

1 Begin by cutting the toe section from the sock.

Toe section   Ankle section

2 Take the ankle section of the sock. Using some white cotton string, tie up the cut end of this section.

Then turn the sock inside out.

3 Filling the sock with rice can be tricky. To make this step easier, slide a roll of tape over the open end of the sock. Then turn the sock down over the roll of tape. This will hold the sock open.

Fill the sock with as much dry rice as will fit.

4 Now tie up the open end of the rice-filled sock.

5 To make the snowman's head, tie another piece of cotton string about one third of the way down the snowman.

Make sure the string is tied very tight.

6 Make the snowman a scarf from a scrap of fabric and tie it around his neck.

If you like knitting, you can even knit a mini woolen scarf for your snowman.

To make the snowman's hat, take the toe section of the sock that you cut off earlier. Turn up the cut edge to make a brim and then pull onto the snowman's head.

Glue three buttons to the snowman's body using the glue gun.

Finally, give your snowman a face using three pins.

MELTED BEAD TREE DECORATIONS

Have fun melting Perler beads to create cool, colorful Christmas tree decorations.

YOU WILL NEED:

- A metal baking sheet
- Baking parchment
- Cookie cutters in Christmas shapes
- Cooking spray
- Small bowl
- Perler beads in your choice of colors
- Oven mitt or potholder
- Wire cooling rack
- Scraps of ribbon

Make sure you are using Perler beads. The packaging must say that the beads are suitable for heating and fusing.

1 Preheat the oven to 350°F (180°C).

2 Place a sheet of baking parchment on the baking sheet.

Baking sheet

Baking parchment

3 Place the cookie cutters on the baking sheet.

4 Now it's time to get creative with the beads!

Try experimenting with different color and pattern combinations. You can put the beads in the small bowl to mix them up and test out your ideas.

5 Spray some cooking spray inside each cookie cutter.

6 Once you've decided on a color combo, place the beads in your chosen cookie cutter shape.

The beads should be one or two beads deep.

Shuffle the cookie cutter to make sure the beads settle in every curve, corner, or point of the cutter.

7 When all the cookie cutters are filled with beads, it's time to get melting. Using an oven mitt or potholder, place the baking sheet into the oven.

8 Leave the beads in the oven for 20 minutes or until the beads have melted and fused together.

9 Remove the baking sheet from the oven. Do not try to remove the beads from the cookie cutters yet. Stand the cookie cutters on a wire rack or heatproof surface to cool for one hour.

10 Once the beads and cookie cutters are completely cold, the bead decorations will slide or pop from the cutters. Wash the cooking spray from the decorations with warm water and dishwashing detergent.

11 Find a small gap or hole in the decoration and thread a ribbon or a piece of string or cord through for hanging.

If there are no gaps, ask an adult to help pierce a small hole for the ribbon using an ice pick.

FABRIC SCRAPS GARLAND

Old T-shirts, jeans, scraps of fabric, and holiday-themed ribbons can easily be turned into this handmade Christmas **garland**.

YOU WILL NEED:

- Fabric and ribbon
- Measuring tape
- Scissors
- String
- String of LED lights

1 Begin by cutting a piece of string to the length you need for your garland.

Tie a loop in one end.

2 Select your fabrics and ribbons. You can buy squares of fabric for quilting from craft stores.

You can also get recycling by cutting up old items such as clothes, tablecloths, or cushion covers. You can even visit thrift stores to cheaply buy items made from colorful, interesting fabrics.

Recycled fabrics

Quilting squares

Ribbon

3 Now cut the fabric into strips that are about 7 inches (18 cm) long and 1.5 inches (4 cm) wide. You will need about 20 fabric or ribbon strips for every 6 inches (15 cm) of garland.

Loop in string

Single knot

4 Begin tying the fabric and ribbon strips to the length of string. All you need to do is tie each strip in a single tight knot.

5 Keep adding fabric and ribbon strips. As you tie each one, push it down the string toward the knot and loop, so they are all bunched up together.

6 Alternate the colors in whatever pattern works for you. When you have completed the garland, tie a knot and loop in the other end to keep the strips from sliding off.

Also, the two loops can be used for hanging your garland.

If you'd like a garland with lights, you can tie your ribbons to a string of LED Christmas lights.

GLOSSARY

creativity
The use of imagination or original ideas to create something new and unusual.

environmentally friendly
Something that does not harm the environment. For example, recycling and reusing materials, such as cardboard or plastic, keeps them from being thrown away and buried in landfill. Also, reusing something stops the need to use raw materials and energy to make new materials or objects.

garland
A length of flowers, leaves, bows, or other items that are strung together and hung up as a decoration.

recycled
Turned into something new instead of being thrown away. For example, old clothes can be recycled into fabric for making new items.

traditional
A way of thinking, behaving, or doing something that a group of people have followed for a long time. For example, the way that people decorate their homes for Christmas can be part of a tradition.

unique
Something that is one of a kind. Handmade objects are unique because each one is different from the next, unlike objects made in a factory.

INDEX

FURTHER INFORMATION

BOOKS:

Handyman, Robyn. *Origami for Christmas.* New York, NY: PowerKids Press, 2017.

Lim, Annalees. *Christmas Crafts.* New York, NY: Windmill Books, 2016.

WEBSITES:

Enchanted Learning: Christmas Theme Page
http://www.enchantedlearning.com/crafts/christmas/
Visit this site to find more fun and festive crafts to make for Christmas!